PREVENTION FOR ALL SEASONS

BY

DR. MYLES H. BADER

PREVENTION INSTEAD OF COSTLY REPAIRS
GRANDPA'S SECRETS TO PROTECTING YOUR PROPERTY

PREVENTION FOR ALL SEASONS

BY

DR. MYLES H. BADER

Printed in the United States of America

ILLUSTRATIONS BY: DEBORAH & RANDY PEEK

TABLE OF CONTENTS

CHAPTER 1

GENERAL SEASONAL TIPS

CAP IT!
There are a number of outside vents that should be capped year round. These include the dryer outlet and the vents on the roof. Most home stores have special caps that will allow the vents to function efficiently while keeping animals and birds out.

MUY IMPORTANTE
In some areas of the country, especially the Southwest, the water is soft and contains chemicals that may affect the growth of certain plants. Discuss this problem with your gardening store if you have soft water coming into your sprinkling system.

BUTTON, BUTTON
Test the ground fault interrupters (GFI) monthly by pressing the test button, which should then cause the reset button to pop out.

PREVENTION TIPS

PREVENTION INSTEAD OF INTERVENTION

SEASONAL PREVENTION
- Air conditioner filters replaced every month during the heavy use months.
- Inspect your yard drains.
- Inspect the house paint regularly and repair as soon as you spot a problem or even just flaking.
- Be sure that sprinklers are adjusted.
- Inspect shingles and shake roofs.
- Check on deck hand rails for stability.

- Check grout between tiles for loose areas and replace.
- Clean dryer duct and the foil opening for any buildup.
- Check hose connections on washer and dryer for minor leaks and replace the hoses every 2 years.

ANNUAL PREVENTION

- Pressure, wash the house, pool cage and any decking.
- Clean the condensation lines on your cooling system.
- Inspect outside air conditioners unit for debris.
- Anode rod in water heater should be inspected.
- Make sure water seal on any deck is still active.
- Check chimney and shroud.
- Be sure and inspect foundation drain openings and clean if necessary.
- Inspect site drainage.
- Lubricate and inspect garage door and springs.
- Replace the thermostat batteries if applicable.
- Inspect thresholds and weather stripping.

THE FATS IN THE FIRE
Check the range vent filter for cleaning. This is a fairly common spot for a fire to start. Twice a year is recommended.

WHERE'S THE TURN OFF
Make sure you know where the water turn off is located for your home so that you can stop a leak immediately. You would be amazed at how many people do not know where it is.

DRAIN ME, DRAIN ME
All garden hoses need to be drained before the first freezing temperatures arrive. Be sure to roll them up and store them properly or you will be buying new ones in the spring.

SIDING PREVENTION TIPS

ALUMINUM, STEEL & VINYL

♦ Aluminum and steel will show scratches and can be dented easily by a rock or other object.

♦ Scratches can be touched up if you saved some paint from the original paint job.

♦ Professionals have methods to remove the dents but it is not easy.

♦ Aluminum and steel need to be grounded at each corner of the building.

♦ Vinyl will not dent and will absorb the shock from most objects thrown at the house.

♦ Vinyl siding can crack and cracked areas should be replaced as soon as the damage is noticed.

♦ Inspect all manufactured siding for loose or damaged sections and especially open seams and joints.

BRICK, BLOCK & STONE

♦ Inspect any brick, block or stone, walls and siding twice a year.

♦ Look for chipped, cracked, loose deteriorating or missing material.

♦ Repair problems to keep water out of masonry material and possibly cause failure or damage.

♦ Check all mortar joints for weak or crumbling mortar.

♦ Use an old screwdriver to test the mortar by scratching along the mortar joints and making sure that the mortar is still firm.

♦ Repair any areas where the mortar is crumbly, cracked or has fallen out or water will enter and cause more damage.

♦ If a white powdery substance has formed on the surface of masonry it is called "efflorescence" and can be washed off. If it returns it may be a sign of water penetrating the wall through cracks or faulty mortar joints or defective caulking or flashing material.

♦ If any area is bulging or has a large crack have it checked by a professional.

STUCCO SIDING

- ♦ Inspect your stucco siding at least once or twice a year. Best to do it before the shrubs and trees start to develop so that you can see all areas easily.
- ♦ Look for hairline cracks and bulges or holes in the stucco.
- ♦ Repair with elasteromeric paint. This is a rubberized paint designed specifically for stucco.

WOOD SIDING

- ♦ Inspect for paint problems twice a year.
- ♦ Repaint every 5 years.
- ♦ Peeling or blistering paint is caused by warm, moist vapor from the house that flows through the walls and reaching the cold sheathing then condensing.
- ♦ Only a few drops of water between the siding and the film of paint will cause the paint to blister and peel off.
- ♦ Install vents if necessary in the siding to handle the moisture problem.
- ♦ Make sure the defective areas are properly prepared and repainted.
- ♦ If you notice other paint problems, such as flaking, wrinkling or "alligator skin" it is best to repaint those areas as soon as possible.
- ♦ Be sure that any untreated wood is not touching the ground or moisture and insects will do damage.
- ♦ A quality stain can protect wood siding from moisture and insect damage. Best to re-stain every 5-7 years.
- ♦ Look for dry rot or termite damage and correct as soon as it is spotted.

CHAPTER 2

SUMMER

CAULK IT OR LOSE IT!
At the beginning of summer you should check all joints for caulking, especially around windows and doors. If you properly seal these areas it will prevent the loss of cool air and allow less warm air to come in. This can result in a substantial savings. Place a bead of caulk along a joint and smooth it out with a wet finger. This will give a nice smooth look and insure complete coverage.

BE A SMOOTHIE
Check all windows and doors to be sure that they move smoothly. Clean the moving parts and lubricate them, as needed using just a light, oil-based lubricant.

WHOOOOOSH
Vacuum all the vents and other heating components as well as the coils on the back of the refrigerator.

GLUB, GLUB, GLUB
During the summer, it would be best to allow the bog garden to flood and become heavily saturated for at least 4-6 weeks. This depends on your climate and the rain during that period.

HOW DO I GET RID OF CONDENSATION ON MY WINDOW FRAMES?
If you have condensation build-up around windows in areas that have high humidity or high temperatures in the summer, try installing a vinyl thermal between the inside and outside of the window frame. If you have drapes on the window leave them open or replace with mini-blinds.

SUMMER STORM APPROACHING
Always be sure that water is draining away from the house during a storm. If the water pools around the foundation it may seep through the walls and dampen the basement. The ground should always slope away from the house about 1-inch for every 4-feet.

SEAL 'EM UP
This is the best time of year to seal and clean your decking. You need to maintain the deck's appearance and make sure you provide protection against the elements. This will prolong the life of the deck and be sure and use the right application material for your type of wood.

ATTIC TIPS

INSULATE & VENTILATE
Be sure that the attic is well ventilated and insulated before cold weather starts to arrive. The rule of thumb is 1 square foot of ventilation for every 300 square feet of attic square footage. However, the ideal is really 1 square foot for every 150 square feet.

LOOK UP! ARE YOU SEEING LIGHT?
One of the best methods of finding leaks in the roof is to go up to the attic and look up to find where any light is showing through. Poke something through the hole so that it will be easy to find when you are on the roof.

CANNED FOAM TO THE RESCUE
Another problem area is where ceiling penetrations are around pipes and wiring. These locations should be sealed up with canned foam insulation.

REDUCE COOLING COSTS
Make sure that the operation of the attic fans and turbine vents are functioning and are in good repair. These help to reduce moisture and heat buildup. They will also help keep your summer cooling costs down. Lubricate where necessary to insure the proper operation.

GOOD MOTION

Best to inspect and install automatic lighting timers and possibly motion detectors. These are important in keeping burglars from entering your property and also to protect your family.

SUMMER CHECK LIST

[ ]   Best to monitor basement humidity and keep the relative humidity under 60%. You can use a dehumidifier to maintain a safe level.

[ ]   Check all basement pipes for condensation or dripping and correct the problem. If the problem exists reduce the humidity with a dehumidifier or insulate the cold water pipes.

[ ]   The basement floor drain (if applicable) should be checked at the beginning of summer to be sure that the trap contains water. If not refill it.

[ ]   Run water in the tap of any plumbing fixture that has not been used in a while to keep water in the trap.

[ ]   The beginning of summer is the best time to deep clean the carpets and rugs from the spring rains and winter grit.

[ ]   The bathroom fan grills should be vacuumed.

[ ]   Be sure and disconnect the duct connected to the dryer and vacuum all the lint out of it as well as all areas around the dryer. Don't forget the dryer vent hood outside.

[ ]   Check the security of all staircase handrails and any guardrails on decking.

[ ]   Check the functioning of all windows and pulleys and lubricate as needed.

[ ]   Check the putty areas around windows on outside of the glass and replace putty as needed.

[ ]   Clean or replace air conditioner filter. This can be done every 1-2 months.

[ ]   Lubricate door hinges and tighten screws if they need it.

[ ]   Check garage door hardware and lubricate or replace as needed.

[   ]   Check the owners manual and lubricate the garage door opening motor, chain and any other moving parts. Be sure that the auto reverse mechanism is working properly.

[   ]   Inspect any electrical service lines for secure attachments where they enter your home and be sure that there is no water leakage into the house along the electrical conduit.

[   ]   Check exterior wood siding and the trim for any signs of deterioration. If you find any, clean replace or refinish the area.

[   ]   Be sure and check for holes in the exterior cladding and seal them off. These are perfect entry points for small pests and insects.

[   ]   Remove any plants, roots or vines that come into contact with or penetrate the siding of the house or any bricks.

[   ]   Use binoculars to check the roof for problems that you can't see from the ground.

[   ]   Repair any cracks in the driveway.

[   ]   Check all steps and be sure that they are in good repair.

SUMMER LANDSCAPE TIPS

- Complete flower installation.
- Turf mowing.
- Turf edging.
- Fertilize azaleas.
- Prune azaleas after bloom drop.
- Bed trimming.
- Shrub pruning as needed.
- Treat diseases as necessary.
- Remove tree suckers.

CHAPTER 3

FALL

GENERAL INFORMATION:

Heating leaks are notorious for causing your winter heating bills to rise. Before the winter hits you need to check any area that may allow outside cold air to enter and seal up or re-weather strip any problem areas.

AIR AROUND THE ELECTRICAL OUTLETS

Hardware stores sell inexpensive foam gaskets that can be placed around the outlets to seal them up. They also have special plastic outlet covers.

STOPPING THE COLD AIR AROUND THE WINDOW UNIT

Window air conditioners should have a cover for the winter that goes inside as well as outside.

ARE FILTERS IMPORTANT IN WINTER?

Filters should be changed twice a year or purchase special filters that can be reused and vacuumed.

CAN HUMIDIFIER BE LEFT ON ALL YEAR

The humidifier should be turned off after the cold season is over.

PADS & FILTERS

The pads or filters in a humidifier will develop scale, especially if you have very hard water and should be replaced every year.

SAT ALL SUMMER, NOW WILL NOT RUN

If the humidifier does not work when turned on after sitting all summer, the float is probably stuck. The float needs to be removed after the winter and cleaned with white vinegar to remove any residue.

CLEAR THE DEBRIS, FLUSH THOSE GUTTERS

Before the winter storms, you should be sure that all the gutters and downspouts are free of all debris and be sure that you have installed metal covers to keep the animals out that are looking for shelter in your attic. Seal up all areas where the seal is not good with tape.

ROOF & CHIMNEY TIPS

GENERAL INFORMATION:

 The chimney needs to be checked before the winter season starts to be sure that the damper is working properly. Check and see if all the bricks are in place and that no mortar has fallen out. Be sure and close the flue after you have used the fireplace to reduce heat loss in the house.

KEEP SANTA'S SUIT CLEAN

Chimneys need to be cleaned to remove soot and creosote after about every third cord of wood. Once a year, however, is about average and should be OK. Best to have a professional do the job for about $45.

SEAL'EM UP

A close inspection of the chimney to be sure that there are no gaps to the pointing is necessary.

BROWN RATS LOVE CHIMNEYS

Best to install a cap on the chimney to keep rats, birds and small animals from getting into the house.

HOW TO MAINTAIN STONE HEARTH & WALL

Hopefully, a layer of penetrating-sealer was applied with tung oil. This is moisture-resistant and will form a coating tough enough to clean. To remove the soot, dissolve 4 ounces of yellow laundry soap in boiling water then allow it to cool.

Add ½ pound of powdered pumice and ½ cup of household ammonia to the mixture and mix well. Use a stiff brush and remove as much soot as possible then apply the mixture with a paintbrush and allow it to remain for ½ hour then wash off with a stiff brush and warm water.

SLATE HEARTH MAINTENANCE

Slate is porous and must be sealed to protect it from scratches, soil and grease. Slate can be cleaned using a mild detergent and water and will not be damaged by harsh cleaners, which are not needed to clean slate.

HOW CAN I BE OLD AT 10

If you have a masonry chimney over 10 years old, it is probably due for inspection by a professional.

Many of the old chimneys are not lined and the mortar between the bricks can break down over the years from heat gasses and wood emissions. Even if you have a clay liner, it can deteriorate and crack over time. These possible problems can cause a chimney fire.

GET OUT THE MAGNIFYING GLASS

- ◆ You will need to get up on the roof and check the shingles to see if there are any that are missing, loose or damaged and replace them.
- ◆ Check all flashing to be sure that it is secure and repair if necessary.
- ◆ Check the area around the nail heads to see if re-caulking is needed.
- ◆ Repair any tears or gaps with roofing cement.
- ◆ Do any re-nailing as needed.

LOOK OUT BELOW

If you are not comfortable being up on the roof, especially if you have a two-story home or a steeply pitched roof call a professional.

BETTER LOSE SOME WEIGHT

Remember that tile and slate shingles can easily be broken by the weight of a person if you step on them wrong. Best to call a professional if you need some replaced.

SAVE THAT SHINGLE

It is always best when you re-shingle a roof to save some of the batch you used if you need to replace some of the shingles due to damage over the years. They will match since they are from the same batch color run. Shingles usually last 15-25 years.

MOSS & MILDEW ALERT

Inspect the roof for moss and mildew on wood shake roofs. Tiny roots from these organisms can penetrate the wood and allow water and the elements to damage the shakes and speed up their decay. This problem can occur on ceramic, slate and cement-fiber tiles as well.

DON'T RUST ON MY ROOF

Be sure and inspect a metal roof for cracks or open joints at the soldered seams. Metal sheets will expand and contract, placing stress on these joints. The stress can break the seal and cause a leak.

TAR & GRAVEL, NOT TAR & FEATHER!

These are roofs that are covered with alternating layers of roofing tar to form a continuous sealed surface then covered with crushed rock or gravel. If you see a blister never step on it since it is usually caused by air or water vapor trapped between layers of the roofing felt. Your weight may crack the roofing felt. Call a professional!

DON'T BE A BAD FLASHER

Very common roof leaks are around flashed areas. Best to repair the flashing before you have to replace the whole roof. Just re-caulk a dried out flashing seam.

SMOKE DETECTOR

BEEP, BEEP, BEEP
If the smoke detector goes off when its not supposed to, there is dust or dirt in the smoke detector. Take it apart and clean it or vacuum it out.

CHANGE ME, CHANGE ME
Batteries in smoke detectors should be changed once a year usually in the fall. Best to place a small piece of tape on the detector with the date that it was last changed.

GARDEN TIPS

◆ Turf mowing.
◆ Turf weed control.
◆ Bed edging and trimming.
◆ Aerate.
◆ Fertilize all turf with high potassium fertilizer.
◆ Begin leaf removal.
◆ Shrub pruning and shaping.
◆ Treat any diseases.
◆ Turn off any irrigation systems and winterize.

GET MY COAT, I'M FREEZING
Many bulbs are very tender and should be removed from the ground before freezing winter temperatures. Bulbs will remain healthier if removed from the ground in almost any climate. If the foliage begins to turn yellow and the plant falls over, it is time to remove it from the ground.

BEST TO BE A "COOL" BULB
Bulbs that are removed from the ground need to be stored in a cool, dry location. Ideally, the temperature should be around 50^0F. When they are removed from the ground, cut the tops back and only allow about 2 inches of the stem to remain. Be sure and remove any traces of soil.

GET OUT THE CLIPPERS
This is the best time to prune your trees and shrubs as well as to fertilize. Lime and aerate the lawn.

TRIM THAT TREE
Make sure that there are no tree limbs touching the house. In a storm they can damage the roof and they are also very handy for small animals (and maybe a few big ones) to get on the roof.

WINTERIZE YOUR IN-GROUND POOL

CLOSING A POOL FOR WINTER

- Locate your supplies that should include the cover, water tubes; plugs for the skimmers and return jets and the winterizing chemicals. You will also need a shop vacuum or air compressor.
- Backwash the filter and be sure its clean. Drain the DE filter tank and leave backwash valve open. On sand filters, unplug the filter drain plug and leave it off. Store the drain plug and other items removed in the pump basket. Be sure that the multiport valve has no water in it. If it does, blow it out. Never use acid to clean the filter before storing it for the winter.
- Disconnect the pump and filter and be sure that the pump has no water left in it. Remove any drain plugs from the pump and store in pump basket.
- If you have a heater, be sure that there is no standing water left inside and remove all drain plugs and blow it out with a compressor or shop vacuum. Leave the heater tray in.
- Loosen any quick disconnect fittings or unions at the pump or filter system. You don't want freeze cracks.
- Remove all return jet fittings (the whole fitting). Remove all skimmer baskets.
- Blow out all return jet pipes using an air compressor. Keep the air blowing until all the air bubbles become visible from the return jets to the pool. Place a plug into the fitting under the water when you see the bubbles blowing out at full force. Be sure that the plug is very tight.

- Blow out the skimmer similar to #7. Place a Gizzmo-type screw plug in the skimmer when bubbles start to become visible. Be sure and place Teflon tape on the Gizzmo threads before installing. You can use black, rubber-type plugs if you prefer over the Gizzmo plug, however, there must be something in the skimmer to allow for water expansion when it freezes.
- You could use a closed empty water bottle. Don't plug the skimmer lines and forget about them since water can easily freeze in a skimmer and crack the plastic. If you have a waterfall, you will have to drain and blow out those pipes as well. If you evacuate your lines properly you will not need to use antifreeze.
- Blow out the main drain line and when you see bubbles coming out of the drain, plug the pipe on your end or close the gate valve. By doing this you will cause an air lock in the line and water will not enter the pipe from the poolside.
- Be sure and place duct tape on all exposed piped to stop anything from getting in them.
- Be sure and remove all floats and rope from pool.
- Place the pump; filter diving board and ladders in a shed. A sand filter can be left in place.
- Make sure that the chemicals bring the pool chlorine level to greater than 3.0 for the winter and the products should consist of a shock-type product.
- Make sure that there are no tears in the pool cover.

GRANDPA HINTS FOR CARING FOR YOUR SOLAR BLANKET

➢ The best way to store a solar blanket is on a roller.
➢ If you need to clean the solar blanket use "solar cover cleaner."
➢ Never leave the solar blanket outside in the winter.
➢ Make sure that the pool is always chemically balanced.
➢ When it starts to flake, buy a new one.

CALL A PRO

Before winter arrives, it would be best to call a heating professional to evaluate and check your system. They will be very busy after the winter hits.

THE RIGHT PROGRAM IS IMPORTANT

Be sure and reprogram your thermostat setting for the winter months at the end of the fall. Remember that standard time will be returning in October.

TEMPERATURE CONTROL

Best not to set your thermostat higher than 72^0F while you are at home and lower the thermostat to 65^0F while you are sleeping or are away from home for any length of time.

CHECK THOSE BASEMENT WINDOWS

Basement windows are often forgotten when checking the house before winter arrives. They should be winterized to avoid cold air getting in.

FALL CHECK LIST

[ ] Be sure to open the furnace humidifier damper if the unit has central air conditioning and clean the humidifier to keep it functioning at optimum efficiency.

[ ] Lubricate circulating pump on the hot water system.

[ ] If you have hot water radiators, be sure and bleed out the air. Make sure that the valve is working freely and lubricate if needed.

[ ] Check the forced air furnace fan belt to see if it has excess wear or is loose or noisy. If so lubricate or replace.

[ ] Clean the fan blades, but be sure and unhook the electricity to the motor first.

[ ] Turn the gas pilot light on (if applicable).

[ ] Heating unit or furnace needs to be inspected and serviced by a qualified company every 2-3 years and every year for an oil or gas furnace.

[ ] Filters should be replaced every month during the winter season.

[ ] The filters in the heat recovery ventilator should be checked every 2 months.

[ ] Vacuum the electric baseboard heater vents to remove any dust and debris (or children's toys).

[ ] Remove the grills on the forced air heating outlets and vacuum inside the ducts and as far as you can reach.

[ ] If the heat recovery ventilator has been shut down for the summer, be sure and clean the filters as well as the core then pour water down the condensate drain to test it.

[ ] Clean the portable humidifier, if you used one.

[ ] Have well water tested for quality. Bacteria testing should be done about every 6 months.

[ ] Remove screens on the inside of casement windows, which will allow air from the heating system to keep the condensation from the window glass.

[ ] Check sump pump and line to ensure proper operation and to be sure that there are no obstructions in the line or leaks.

[ ] Replace all window screens with storm windows. Check the caulking on the storm windows.

[ ] Be sure that all doors to the outside shut tightly and check them for ease of use. Replace any worm weatherstripping.

[ ] If you have a door between the house and the garage, be sure and check the self-closing devise to make sure that it will close the door securely.

[ ] Be sure that all windows and skylights close properly.

[ ] Place a cover outside of air conditioner unit.

[ ] Make sure that the ground around the home slopes away from the foundation wall so that water will not drain into the basement.

[ ] Clean leaves from the eaves and the roof.

[ ] Test the downspouts to be sure they are not clogged.

[ ] Check the chimney to be sure a bird has not made a nest in it.

[ ] Drain and store outdoor hoses.

[ ]   Close the valve to any outdoor hose connection and be sure and drain the hose bib unless your home has "frost-proof" hose bibs.

[ ]   If you have a septic tank, be sure and measure the sludge and scum so that you can determine if the tank needs to be emptied before spring. Pump tanks out at least every 3 years.

[ ]   Winterize landscaping by protecting young trees or bushes.

[ ]   Store and cover outdoor furniture.

CHAPTER 4

WINTER

WINTERIZING A HOME

KEEP MY PIPES WARM
Be sure and insulate your pipes if you live in a cold climate. Insulation will go a long way to prevent freeze-ups. You will need to cover every square inch of pipe including the connections. You can purchase pipe jacketing in standard lengths that can easily be cut with a knife. Secure it with electrical tape. If you prefer you can use standard insulation and just cut it to the length you need and tape it securely.

FILL THOSE CAVITIES
At the end of many pipe runs there is an area that may be a small cavity. Be sure and stuff insulation in all open cavities regardless how small the opening may appear to be. Be sure and don't compress the insulation too much or it will not be as effective.

SOMETHING NEW ON THE HORIZEN
When trying to keep pipes warm, try using heat tape. This is electrically charged tape that draws only a fraction of power and is safe and inexpensive. Just wrap the tape around the pipe and then plug the tape into an outlet. The tape contains a thermostat, which turns the tape on and off as needed. The only drawback is that the tape will not work during a power outage.

PROTECT YOUR HOSE BIB
Before winter arrives, be sure and remove all hoses and drain them of all water. Allow all water to drain out of the hose bib (sill cock) and leave it open.

If you do not have an indoor shutoff, it would be best to install one or install a freeze-proof sill cock. Newer homes may have these already installed since many local codes require them.

TRICKLE, TRICKLE
To prevent a problem on very cold days and especially nights, turn on any faucet that you are concerned about and let the water just trickle out continuously. If there is a cabinet underneath, open the doors and allow warm air to enter.

WINTER LAWNCARE TIPS

- ◆ Final leaf removal at start of winter.
- ◆ Tree rising of the limbs and support from snow accumulations.
- ◆ Weed and deadhead flowers as needed.
- ◆ Round up fescue in Bermuda turf and scalp Bermuda turf.
- ◆ Prune myrtle
- ◆ Pine straw mulch application (if applicable).
- ◆ Fertilize fescue.
- ◆ Final deep pruning of shrubs.

WINTERIZING FOR EXTENDED PERIOD

When closing a home or cabin down for the winter, it is not necessary to leave the heat on to avoid a problem. Utilities can safely be turned off if the house is properly prepared with no damage, taking place. You will need to have the water shut off and drain the entire system making the plumbing system dormant.

CALL THE WATER DEPARTMENT
The first thing to do is to call the local water department and ask them to turn off your water to the property. They may just tell you to go to the valve on the street and do it yourself.

OPEN SESAME

The next step is to open all faucets in the home, starting at the top of the system. Shut down and then drain the water heater. Detach all drain hoses on the washing machine and dishwasher.

If you have a drainable valve or two (usually near the water meter) open the drain cock on each and drain the supply lines completely. If you locate a low-lying pipe that doesn't have a faucet or drain cock, just open a union where two pipes join and allow any water to leave.

ANTIFREEZE YOUR TOILET

You will need to replace the water in your toilets with antifreeze solution (use non-toxic antifreeze mixed with water according to directions on container). Place the liquid into the bowl and it should start a mild flushing action with some of the antifreeze remaining in the bowl and toilet trap.

TRAP THAT ANTIFREEZE

Next you will need to pour the antifreeze solution into all fixtures that have a trap, which includes all sinks, showers, bathtubs and even the washing machine standpipe. If the house has a main house trap, you will need to fill the elbow portion with full strength antifreeze for maximum protection.

GOODBYE WINTER, HELLO SPRING

After winter is over its time to get the house back in working condition and reverse everything you did.

- ❖ First, turn all faucets off, including all sill cocks. Best to remove all aerators on faucets and clean them out.
- ❖ You will have to reconnect all the pipes you disconnected and close down all drainable valves.
- ❖ Replace any hoses you removed.
- ❖ Have the water company turn on the water supply.
- ❖ Be sure and turn on all the faucets slowly and begin at the sill cock. The water will spit out for a while getting any air out of the system before a normal flow starts.
- ❖ Be sure and replace the aerators.

DRIP, DRIP, DRIP

If your worried about your water lines freezing just leave one of the taps running very slightly to avoid the problem. If you have a two-story house, open one on the first floor.

CURING FROZEN PIPES

If the pipe has not burst already and you need to find the location of the frozen clog, just swab along the suspect pipe with a damp cloth until frost forms on the area as you pass over it.

WINTER STORAGE

Be sure and wipe down any furniture that has plastic strapping with a solution of baking soda and water before putting them away. Sprinkle it directly on hammocks and canvas chairs as well.

A BIT CHILLY

If you run your air conditioner for 4-6 minutes during the winter it will keep the seals in good shape for the summer.

I'VE GOT YOU UNDER MY SKIN..........................

When you get fiberglass fibers under and on your skin, gently pat the area with fresh duct tape to remove them. Wash the area well after you remove them, with warm soapy water.

COLD AIR COMING UNDER THE DOOR

Because of carpeting, it is necessary to have room under the door so that they will close and not hit the carpet. You will need to install a door sweep, which works by lifting up whenever the door is closed, keeping the warm air in and the cold air out.

OH MY! MY METAL IS EXPOSED

If you are going to leave metal furniture out during the rain or in the winter, be sure and put a coat of automobile wax on all metal surfaces to protect it from rust.

WAX ON, WAX OFF
A coating of car wax on the painted metal surfaces of vinyl furniture will help to protect it.

GETTING COLD, COVER ME UP
Purchase a winter cover for a hot tub that will not allow any water to leak in from rain or snow. If you have a hard cover with a hinged center, you will need to place a vinyl cover over it.

REPLACING THE FILTER
Filters are only good for about one year.

INSULATION

GENERAL INFORMATION:
Basement insulation is lacking in most homes and the average well insulated home in the United States and Canada loses about 1/5th of its total heating bill to the basement walls and the air surrounding the basement. The average homeowner can save $120-150 per year on their heating cost if they insulate the basement.

HEAT LOSS IN THE BASEMENT
Insulating the basement is fairly easy and should cost about $150. Best to talk to a professional at a store that sells insulation for their recommendations and materials.

BRRRRRRRRRRR
Ice and/or snow may affect the fuel lines. The outside lines should be protected against ice or snow that may fall from a roof or tree.

 # FURNACES

GENERAL INFORMATION:

Your furnace does need to be serviced every year for optimal efficiency. Have the servicing done in the late summer or early fall, which should include a cleaning and general tune-up.

If you use oil, the tank should be filled in late summer to avoid the winter costs of heating oil. Having the furnace cleaned can increase the furnace efficiency by as much as 25%.

BURNER MAINTENANCE A MUST

The feeder tubes that enter the control valves located ahead of the burner should be cleaned at the beginning of every season. Spider webs and small dirt particles will clog these very easily and hamper the gas flow to the burners. It can even be a potential fire hazard. If the flames are yellowish and flow slowly, there may be a problem and a clog.

The heat is created in a furnace by burning gas or oil inside the furnace. The hot gasses then pass through the curved metal tubing called a heat exchanger then out of your home through a plastic or metal vent pipe. While this is occurring, the air circulates through your home passing over the outside of a "heat exchanger" and takes on the heat from the hot metal. This warm air is then circulated through your home.

WHERE OH WHERE DID MY OIL PIPE GO?????

If the snow gets too deep, you may have a problem finding your oil pipe for a delivery. Just place a colored flag on a stick that is anchored next to the oil delivery pipe so that the deliveryman can easily find the pipe.

FURNACE DIFFERENCES

Two-Speed Furnace – These furnaces can run on low speed up to 90% of the time and operate more quietly and will run for longer periods of time than single-speed furnaces.

This means fewer drafts caused by frequent on and off cycles. The temperature tends to remain more constant.

Variable-Speed Furnace – These provide the ultimate combination of comfort, efficiency and they are quiet. They are one-step above the two-speed furnace since they offer "smart" motors that monitor your home and adjust the volume and speed of the air providing the most efficient heating and cooling. They also provide significant energy savings.

DOES MY FURNACE HAVE A FILTER?

This depends on the type of furnace you have. If you have a warm air furnace, you have an air filter. If you have a boiler with radiators then you probably don't have a filter.

Most furnace manufacturers place inexpensive fiberglass filters in their furnaces, which remove most airborne particles that might damage the fan and heating coil. However, it is better to have the more expensive filters, which can improve the air quality in the home and remove pollens, mold spores and bacteria.

Pleated filters last from 3-9 months. Disposable fiberglass panel or electrostatic filters should be changed every 1 to 3-months. If you don't change the filters regularly, you will cause the furnace to work harder.

DIRTY FILTER = DIRTY HOME

You can spend less time cleaning and dusting if you change your filters regularly. Duct cleaning is also important and should be done by a professional. The cost is usually from $75-$300 depending on the size of the home. It is also a must if someone has allergies.

GRANDPA TROUBLESHOOTS AN ELECTRIC FURNACE

I'll find the problem

Not getting heat
The furnace switch or the main breaker may be open or the thermostat is set too low for it to turn on. Be sure and check the switch and fuse or breakers and the setting on the thermostat.

Cycling on & off too often
The furnace may have a clogged filter or the blower may be going bad causing the unit to overheat. Try replacing the filter and lubricate the blower.

Not getting enough heat
The thermostat setting is not set right, defective heating element or you have a clogged filter or duct. First check the thermostat setting then check the fuse or breaker. If the fuse or breaker trips when re-set, call a serviceman.

GRANDPA TROUBLESHOOTS A GAS FURNACE

No heat
The thermostat may be set too low or the switch, fuse or circuit breaker may be open. The gas may be shut off or the pilot is out.

The furnace is cycling too often
This is usually caused by; a clogged filter or there is something wrong with the blower. Try replacing the filter and adjust the blower.

Not getting enough heat
Either a clogged filter or the burners need to be cleaned. Replace the filters and have the burners cleaned by a professional and not grandpa.

The blower will not shut off
The fan switch is probably set for continuous circulation or the limit control is out of adjustment. Re-set the fan switch on the furnace or wall or adjust the limit control.

The furnace is squeaking and rumbling

The squealing noise may be from the blower belt slipping or the bearing may need lubrication. If there is rumbling with the burners off it is usually a misadjusted pilot. If there is rumbling with the burners on it usually means that the burners are dirty. Just oil the blower and adjust the belt. Adjust the pilot ands if the burners need cleaning; it should be done by a professional.

Pilot light out at end of season

Be sure and put out the pilot light at the end of the season. It will save you energy and actually prevent rust. Water vapor has the tendency to condense on the surface of the heat exchanger and promote rust.

GRANDPA TROUBLESHOOTS AN OIL FURNACE

It's usually the burner

Burner's don't run

The thermostat setting may be too low or the main switch, circuit breaker or fuse is open. The motor may be overheated. Try setting the thermostat 5^0F higher than your normal setting. Check the switches, breakers and fuses or possibly the motor needs oiling. Check for any reset switches.

Burner's are running but won't fire up

Possibly either the oil or the spark is not getting to the unit or the safeties may be sooty. Be sure all oil valves are open and that there is oil in the tank, best not to trust the gauge. Dip a rod into the tank and check it. Clean the safeties!

Burners are cycling too frequently

You may have a clogged air blower motor or it needs oiling. Replace the filter and oil and adjust limit control.

Burner is squealing & smoking

The combustion air blower motor probably needs oiling. Be sure and shut off unit and allow it to cool then fill the oil cups and check them again after the motor has run for about an hour.

The chimney is smoking
A cold flue may cause this problem when the burner is first fired. If the smoking persists, it's a sign of incomplete combustion, which there is fuel being wasted in the unit.

GRANDPA TROUBLESHOOTS A HEAT PUMP

Heat pump is not running
Either there is no power getting to the unit or the thermostat is not asking for heat.

First check the thermostat setting then the electrical disconnect switch and the fuses or breakers in the circuit panel. Best to also check the reset switch in the outdoor cabinet.

Short cycles are occurring
There may be an obstruction blocking the outdoor coil or possibly the blower unit is not working properly. A clogged filter will also cause the problem. Clear the outdoor coil and check the filter and the blower unit.

Having long or frequent defrost cycles
If the outdoor coil is blocked, it could cause the problem of defrosting that lasts longer than 15 minutes or occurring more than twice an hour. See previous answer.

Getting uneven heating
The heat pomp is putting out a cooler flow of air than you are used to. Also, the indoor temperature will normally drop 2^0F to 3^0F when the outside temperature reaches the system's balance point differential. This is the point when the backup heating should kick in. You can minimize the airflow discomfort by balancing the duct system to offset the balance point differential. However, you may have to raise the thermostat setting during cold weather.

NOT OPERATING PROPERLY
If it an outside unit, it may be obstructed by bushes or trash.

EXCESS WATER DRIPPING FROM HEAT PUMP
The unit is probably iced up and is in the process of defrosting. This is normal.

WATER ON WINDOWPANES
Too much humidity in the home! Turn on an exhaust fan if you have one. Possibly too much plant watering or steam ironing.

GRANDPA TROUBLESHOOTS A STEAM BOILER

Where's the heat?
There is probably no power to the unit; no water or you have a burner problem. First, check the thermostat, switches, breakers or fuses then the water level and make sure that the burners are working properly.

Not enough heat
You may have rust and scale in the boiler and it needs to be flushed. This will constrict the passages and will lower the efficiency. There may also be a buildup on the heating surfaces of soot from combustion; however, this job is for a professional.

Water level keeps getting too low
You may have a leaky return line; call a plumber, however, if there is a leak within the boiler it will require a major repair.

Glass gauges are getting cloudy
The glass may just need cleaning or the boiler needs to be flushed. To clean the gauges, just turn off the boiler and close all valves then loosen the nuts above and below the glass. Lift up the glass and remove it, clean it and replace it.

There are ghosts in my pipes
If you have a problem with noisy pipes, it is probably water trapped in the return lines or in the return main. First check the pitch of all returns and make sure that they slope back toward the boiler. You may need to adjust the slant with new pipe hangers.

WINTER CHECK LIST

[ ]   Heat recovery ventilation systems should be checked at least every 2 months.

[ ] Check your owners manual for your hot water tank and properly drain off some of the water from the clean out valve at the bottom of the tank. This will help control sediment and increase efficiency.

[ ] Check the hot water in the house to see if the water is heating up to the set temperature on the hot water heater.

[ ] The humidifier should be cleaned 2-3 times during the winter.

[ ] Vacuum all bathroom vent grills every 2-3 months.

[ ] Vacuum around all fire and smoke detectors. Dust and cobwebs can prevent them from working, they can also be a home for small insects.

[ ] Clean or replace furnace air filters every month during winter.

[ ] Vacuum the grills on the back of the refrigerator and free-standing freezer. Be sure and empty the drip trays.

[ ] Check the gauges on any fire extinguishers and replace or re-charge as needed.

[ ] Check fire escape routes and have a family emergency drill. Purchase escape ladder if you live in a two-story home.

[ ] Check the basement floor trap and be sure that the trap has contains water. Refill it with water if needed.

[ ] Monitor the home for excessive moisture levels such as checking for condensation on the windows.

[ ] Check all faucets for dripping problems and replace washers if needed. If they require frequent replacement then it would be best to replace the fixture.

[ ] Run some water out of any plumbing fixture that is not used frequently, such as a laundry tub or pool shower to keep water in the trap.

[ ] Clean drains in shower stall, dishwasher, sinks and bathtubs.

[ ] Know where the plumbing shut-off valve is and test it to be sure that it works properly.

[ ] Check all windows and doors for ice accumulation or cold air leaks. Repair in the spring.

[ ] Check attic for frost accumulation and roof for ice dams or icicles. Call a professional for assistance if these occur.

[ ] Examine all electrical cords and outlets for both indoor and outdoor seasonal lighting to ensure fire safety. If the plugs or cords feel warm to the touch it would be best to replace them as soon as possible.

CHAPTER 5

SPRING

BE A LOOKIE-LOO

The spring is the time to get up on the roof and check for winter damage. Snow and ice are hard on your roof and can damage shingles. As soon as the snow is gone and the roof is dry, check it out good. It may even be wise to have a roofing company check out the roof.

HERE A SIDE, THERE A SIDE

After the winter all the siding should be checked for damage. If there is any missing or loose siding it can allow for moisture to get behind the other siding and into the house causing damage.

JUST A LITTLE OFF THE SIDES

Be sure and trim back tree branches and shrubs in the spring that are close to the house or touching the roof. These will cause damage to the shingles and make a mess in the gutters as well as making it easy for animals and insects to reach the house. Shrubs that are growing too close to the house and are too thick can trap moisture and possibly ruin your siding and make foundation problems.

THE SPRING INSPECTOR

This is the time to inspect basement or crawl space walls for potential leaks. Remember, excess moisture in the basement can lead to structural damage and may cause wood floors to buckle on the level above. Check any cracks carefully for any sign of leakage.

GLUB, GLUB

Inspect all water supply lines and valves leading to sinks and toilets for leaks. Repair as soon as possible to save water and damage to any flooring. If there is a leak, shut off the valve to stop the leak until it is fixed. Pipes and drains also need to be checked and if leaks are found cover them with duct tape until the plumber arrives.

WHOOOOPS! SINK HOLE ALERT

Time to inspect the driveway, sidewalks and patio for cracks and any sign of deterioration. Even a minor crack will allow water to soften the ground below resulting in additional cracking. Use concrete calk if the cracks are less than ¼". Use a high-pressure hose to do a good job then make sure that it dries thoroughly before caulking. For larger cracks use concrete patch.

AIR IT OUT!

Best to have your air conditioner serviced at the beginning of spring if you want it to operate at maximum efficiency in the summer months.

THERE ARE SPOTS EVERYWHERE!

These spots are mildew and they form on areas that are damp or areas that receive little or no sunlight. Lower quality paints will also cause this to happen more frequently or painting over a surface that has mildew already on it, which frequently happens. If you are not sure if its mildew or not: try placing a small amount of household bleach on the area. If it bleaches away, its mildew!

WRONG TIME OF YEAR TO PAINT

If your house paint is looking crinkly and has a "skin" on it, the paint was probably applied too thickly last summer. It was probably applied during very hot weather or the humidity was too high. Another cause is that the primer was not cured enough before it was painted over. Scrape and sand off the paint to remove the wrinkled surface and be sure and allow enough time for the primer to dry adequately before applying a coat of paint.

SEPTIC TANKS

GENERAL INFORMATION:

Spring is the best time to be sure that the septic tank is working at its optimum. The septic tank is a large metal tank that sits underground on your property and accumulates your household wastes. Most people do not know how to maintain the tank and problems will occur. There are also natural failures that can occur if the ground fails where the tank is located. Septic systems can cost up to $20,000 to replace if not cared for. Every year about 1200 people die from contaminated water and failed septic systems.

SOIL GETTING PLUGGED WITH SOLIDS

The washing machine causes more septic system failures than almost any other problem area. The problem is the amount of lint, polyester and nylon particles that pass through the filter and end up clogging the pores of the soil drain lines. Your filter only traps 5% of these minute particles.

This problem can be solved, by purchasing an inline filter; which is called a "Septic Protector" and attaches to the washers discharge hose costing about $150.

SOIL BEDS PLUGGED BACKING UP INTO THE SYSTEM

Never do more than 1-2 laundry loads a day to reduce the amount of water going into the septic tank.

ENOUGH ALREADY

Be sure and have a very efficient water softener that will not put too much water into the system every day.

KEEP IT ACTIVE

Septic tanks will be kept in good working order if you keep the bacteria at a high level. Just mix 2 envelopes of active dry yeast with 1 pound of brown sugar in a large bowl then add 4 cups of warm tap water. Mix it up and blend well then allow it to remain in a warm location for about 15 minutes or until foamy and the volume increases. Flush the mixture down the toilet or just buy a commercial activator.

THE EFFLUENT IS BEING KILLED BY HOUSEHOLD CLEANERS

Replace the bacteria in the tank regularly since the household cleaners may be killing them off. Products are available in most supermarkets.

I'M GETTING SICK, PUMP ME OUT

Have the tank pumped every 2-3 years.

SPECIAL FILTER

Effluent filters should be installed (by a professional) in the exit baffle to stop larger solids from clogging the drain field lines.

CHLORINE IS KILLING ME

Using oxygen bleach will help your system stay healthy. The oxygen bleach works better than other types of bleach.

NOTE:
Divert other runoff from roofs, patios and driveways away from your drain field.

SPRINGTIME IS WELL-TESTING TIME

Test your wells at least every 2 years unless you notice an off odor or odd taste. If you have a well, try to eliminate using as many pesticides and fertilizers you can around your property. Be careful throwing chemicals down the drain if you are on a septic tank and a well. Be sure that the top of your well is sealed so that contaminants cannot enter.

CHECKING YOUR OWN TAP WATER

Hints that will help you evaluate you own tap water for possible contamination or problems:

- If your sink has a dark reddish-colored stain it may be the result of rust in your pipes.
- If your sink has greenish stains it is probably from copper leaching from the pipes.
- If you notice a rotten egg smell, it's probably hydrogen sulfide produced from bacteria.
- If the water is cloudy it can be from dirt particles, iron, or bacterial contamination. Cloudy water can also result from small air bubbles forming when the water is under pressure as it leaves the tap and soon dissipates. This is harmless and no need for concern.

OPENING UP A POOL AFTER WINTER

The following is a step-by-step opening process:
1. Be sure and thoroughly clean the area around the pool before removing any covers to minimize the amount of debris that might get into the pool.

2. Basically, just reverse the winterizing procedures and remember to lubricate all bolts on the dive board, ladders and rails.

CLOSE THE FIREPLACE FLUE

Late spring is the time to be sure that the flue is closed on the fireplace to prevent warm air from reducing the efficiency of your air conditioning.

OPENING UP A VACATION HOUSE

PLAYING IT SAFE

When you restore the plumbing system, fill the water heater before turning on the power to it or lighting the pilot light.

GARDEN TIPS FOR SPRING

- ◆ Final mulch application.
- ◆ Rose bush pruning.
- ◆ Remove dead limbs from small trees.
- ◆ High nitrogen turf fertilizing.
- ◆ Shrub pruning as needed.
- ◆ Inspect trees and shrubs for insect damage.
- ◆ Start spring flower installation.
- ◆ Turf and bed trimming

SPRINGTIME IS WEEDTIME

Weeds love the spring and will occupy any opening in your lawn. You need to plant grass seed (If you didn't do it in autumn) in any bare or thinning areas before the weeds have a chance to take over.

TIMBERRRRRRRRRRRRR

Early spring is the best time to clear the yard of downed tree branches and debris left over from the winter. If you leave these items on the lawn it may kill the grass as well as other damage. The earlier you clear branches, leaves and other debris, the healthier your lawn will be for the summer.

PLANT RIGHT OR USE SUNTAN LOTION

Begonias will bloom all summer until the first frost. They can be any color except blue, even two-toned ones. Remember to always stalk begonias. If they get more than 3 hours of morning sun they may burn, so check the area carefully before you plant them.

I'M REALLY PRETTY IN THE FALL

Crocuses will usually bloom in the spring but are not as pretty. If you wait until the early fall you will see nicer flowers appearing. Best to plant the bulbs in late summer and allow them to bloom in the early fall initially.

MULCHING TIME AGAIN

Mulches are the best method of maintaining even soil temperatures in the summer months. They are important, especially in the heat of the day, keeping the soil an even temperature.

VARIETIES OF MULCH:

BUCKWHEAT HULLS

These are lightweight and will not blow away easily. They have the ability to retain moisture very well but are expensive mulch.

COCOA SHELLS

If they become too moist, you may end up with mushrooms. Recommended for flowerbeds. Expensive mulch. Never apply more than one-inch because of its high potash content.

LEAVES

One of the best mulches for adding nutrients and keeping the soil in shape! Keeps the soil moist and cool. Should be shredded for the best results.

PINE NEEDLES

Do not retain moisture very well.

SHREDDED BARK

Comes in different grades. Use the coarser grades for under large shrubs and the finer grades for flowerbeds. Reasonably priced.

WOOD CHIPS

Only use aged wood chips or shavings since wood chips remove nitrogen from the soil. Aged wood chips are best since they will break down and add organic matter to the soil.

SPRING CHECK LIST

[ ]   Have fireplace, woodstove or chimney cleaned and inspected at least once a year.

[ ]   Shut down and clean furnace humidifier and close the humidifier damper on any unit that has central air conditioner.

[ ]   The air conditioner system should be checked and serviced every 2-3 years by a professional.

[ ]   Clean or replace air conditioner filter (if applicable).

[ ]   Check dehumidifier and clean and service if needed.

[ ]   Turn off any gas furnace and fireplace pilot lights (if applicable).

[ ]   Check your hot water manual and test the temperature and pressure relief valve to be sure that it is not stuck. **Be careful since this test may release hot water that can burn you.**

[ ]   Test well water every 6 months for quality.

[ ]   Check the smoke detector, carbon monoxide and security alarms and replace batteries once a year.

[ ]   Clean all the windows, screens and hardware and replace the storm windows with screens that are in good repair.

[ ]   Check screens and replace or repair as needed.

[ ]   Open the valve to all outside hose connections after the last possible frost has passed.

[ ]   Examine the foundation and walls of the house for cracks, leaks or signs of moisture damage and repair if needed.

[ ]   Paint any fencing as needed.

[ ]   Check any garden stone pathways for winter damage and replace if needed.

[ ]   Place new sealer on all decking (if applicable).

[   ]   Be and check to see if the sump pump is working properly before the spring thaw sets in. Be sure that the discharge pipe is connected and that water is draining away from the foundation.

[   ]   Re-level any exterior steps or decking that may have moved due to settling or frost.

[   ]   Check eaves and downspouts for loose joints and be sure that all the attachments are secure. Check for any obstructions.

[   ]   Be sure and clear any drainage ditches or culverts of debris.

[   ]   Fertilize young trees and do any spring landscaping cleanup and planting.

CHAPTER 6

VACATION DO'S & DONT'S

VACATION HOUSE CLOSURE FOR THE WINTER

Before you close up your vacation house for the winter, drain the plumbing to prevent freeze-ups. Tell the water company to shut off the water supply and close the main valve. Open up all faucets starting with the top floor and be sure and open all outside faucets as well.

Flush all toilets and pour plumbing fixture anti-freeze into each bowl and sink trap. Follow the directions on the package.

KA-BOOM
If you leave home for an extended vacation, be sure to open all the hot water taps for a few minutes when you first enter the house to release any possible hydrogen gas that may have been building up in the hot water heater.